Free From Captivity

Free From Captivity

by James Alford

Free From Captivity

Copyright © 2015 by James Alford

This book may be freely distributed or quoted as long as contents retain their biblical meaning and spiritual value. All Rights Reserved for any other use.

ISBN-13: 978-0988764620
ISBN-10: 0988764628

Righteousness Ministries c/o
Righteousness Publishing

www.righteousnessministries.org
www.kingdomauthority.org
Email: info@righteousnessministries.org

Printed in U.S.A

This book is dedicated to those who desire to live an abundant life in Jesus Christ.

Contents

Preface..9

1. Born in Chains...................................11

2. Reality of the Spirit Realm.................29

3. Improper Births................................39

4. The Children's Bread........................57

5. The Abundant Life...........................67

6. Purposed to Pour into Others...........85

7. Dead Weight....................................91

8. Fruits of Liberty.............................101

FREE FROM CAPTIVITY

Preface

    When most people think of captivity they think of someone or something that has been physically bound in chains or behind bars. The word captivity brings thoughts of criminals being in prison or even of past times where peoples around the world were sold from person to person with no hope of liberty. Most people that are in physical captivity these days is because they have been convicted of a crime. If you look at the history of man's existence on this earth over the last few of thousand years you'll see that many were born into a state of slavery and others were sold into it. Many peoples condition was the end product of some type of warfare or conflict that ended in defeat for the side they were on. Some became quite comfortable and embracive of their condition and others lived for the opportunity to be free. Some would escape and quickly realize that they would rather be captive and others killed themselves choosing death over living in chains.

Even in today's society people fight for freedom from many different oppressions, and although it may not be as confining as times in the past, to be captive is never what man was intended by God to be. God created man to be free from oppression, free from sickness, free from sin, free from hurt and sadness, free from torment; and yet mankind suffers from all these. On the news we see Christian churches being burnt down constantly across the world. In some places it is illegal to even talk to people about Jesus. We see countries were religious liberties used to be the norm now compromised.

It is a treacherous reality that our adversary, Satan is working around the clock to take us into a state of captivity...Mind, Body, and Spirit. The bible even says in 1Peter 5:8 *"Be sober, be vigilant; because your adversary the devil, as a roaring lion, walketh about, seeking whom he may devour:"*. Satan tried to enslave the whole world through the mistake Adam and Eve made. Now, with the power of Jesus, and our ability to be free from sin and death, Satan works overtime to disguise the reality of captivity in people's lives and the availability of freedom in Jesus Christ.

This book takes the reader down the various paths that lead to spiritual captivity in peoples lives. Then it examines how to get free and stay there.

Chapter 1
Born In Chains

John 8:32 And ye shall know the truth, and the truth shall make you free.

<u>Natural Chains</u>

It must have been a shock to the slaves in North America when the people started saying that they were free. For some all they had ever known was that they were owned by someone. They were required to eat when told to eat, sleep when told to sleep, and work as long as it pleasured the ones that owned them. Their life was captive to another...Not even having the right to keep their own children, husbands, and wives. While some where used to being enslaved, most knew that it wasn't right. It was not what man was meant to be. It is in man's nature to be free.

    Many rebellions and wars have been fought to

free a people. Many times these people had at one point of time in the past been in bondage. In Bible times, whole nations where enslaved as a result of war. The nation of Israel in particular many times found itself in a place of physical bondage. God being faithful to them would deliver them out of their captivity.

One of the more known stories in the bible about a people being enslaved, then delivered, is when the nation of Israel was held captive in Egypt. The bible said that God heard the suffering of the people and he agreed to free them. He first told Moses to go to the Pharaoh of Egypt and request their release. Once this initial request was denied, God began to show how serious he was to deliver this nation of people out of captivity. God sent multiple signs and plagues to guarantee the deliverance of Israel. By the time that Pharaoh and the nation of Egypt had suffered all the plagues, it was painfully obvious that God was not going to stop until Israel was free.

After the nation of Israel was allowed to walk out of Egypt, the soldiers of Egypt began to chase them. God allowed the sea to be parted and the people of Israel were allowed to walk to the other side. As soon as the last of the people reached the other side, God closed the waters around the soldiers that followed them. God had secured an absolute freedom for them.

In today's society, physical captivity is used to deter crime. Society knows that being controlled and restricted is punishment and will stop many from breaking the laws that have been set in place. I have yet to hear a person say that they enjoyed going to prison. Most will tell you it is a terrible place.

Natural Captivity can come from four sources, it can come from our society as a whole, own selves, Satan, or God. All four have different reasons and goals to be accomplished from the captivity. Society places people in to captivity because they have committed a crime or have done something to the disliking of the society they are a part of. Millions are held in prisons around the world because they were found guilty of violating the laws of the nation they were in. Some of those who are in these prisons absolutely deserve to be there and others are victims of the system that is in place.

We always like to think of God as a liberator and champion of freedom, but sometimes God allows for people to become captive naturally so that they may be spiritually free. God allowed for Jonah to be swallowed by the large fish because he was disobedient in following the direction of God. The bibles says that Jonah was held there for three days and when he was ready to follow the direction of God, he was released back on the sea shore.

Satan also has his brand of natural captivity. Satan places people into natural captivity to stop the work of God and discourage the man or woman of God. Satan worked very hard to put the Apostle Paul into prison many times for preaching the Gospel of Jesus Christ. Even today in certain countries we hear on the news about people being placed in prison because they are talking to people about Jesus or even just for the mere fact of being a Christian. Jesus said in Revelations 2:10 *"Fear none of those things which thou shalt suffer: behold, the devil shall cast some of you into prison, that ye may be tried; and ye shall have tribulation ten days: be thou faithful unto death, and I will give thee a crown of life."*

Satan, God, and society are not the only sources of natural captivity. People can place themselves in natural captivity. While many times the captivity that people place themselves in works hand in hand with the breaking of the laws of the land, individuals can for all manner of reasons cut themselves off from life and others for one reason or another. Some people that close themselves away from others are victims of their own captivity.

Spiritual Captivity

Natural captivity places unnatural conditions on the physical movement of a man or woman. While natural captivity is a place of despair and discontentment. There is a captivity that goes beyond natural bondage. While natural captivity is the place that seems to be the worst state, there is one that is a far more entangling and destructive state. Natural bondage is always a temporary place. If a person stays in jail for the rest of their natural life, there is some liberty in a physical death, and while death may not sound liberating, for the Christian it is a transition to eternal life of joy and communion with God. There is however a bondage that transcends time and space sometimes resulting in an eternal state. It can cut off salvation and lead to an eternity of pain, despair, and misery. It is called Spiritual Captivity.

As human beings we have three components... body, soul, and a spirit. (1 Thessalonians 5:3) Your body is your physical self. Your soul is your mind and the object of salvation. Your spirit is the plug that God plugs his spirit into so that you can have a relationship with him. Spiritual captivity can affect and put in bondage all three. When people are put in jail, sometimes they are wrongly convicted and sentenced to long times in jail and some are even sentenced to death. We see on the news all the time, people being found innocent after spending many years in prison. Just as in the natural, people are put in spiritual bondage even though they may be innocent. It's easy to recognize that someone is behind bars, but many times it is hard to determine that someone is spiritually captive. I equate spiritual captivity as something of a silent killer, "you seem to be free but in actuality you are dying on the inside." It is far more dangerous in all aspects of our existence. Jesus said in, Rev 3:17 *"Because thou sayest, I am rich, and increased with goods, and have need of nothing; and knowest not that thou art wretched, and miserable, and poor, and blind, and naked:"*. We understand by this scripture that Jesus was saying that people look at their natural circumstances but have no idea of their spiritual condition. In the example Jesus gave, the person thought because they were well off in the natural and having a level of success, everything was in a good place, but it is obvious that natural perceptions can confuse the true condition of a person.

Origins of Spiritual Captivity

Spiritual Captivity can come from two sources. It can come from our own carnal selves or from the work of the devil. God will not bring you into a state of spiritual captivity because any commitment you make to God is of a willing and voluntary nature. Many years ago I had a woman call me about an issue she was having with God. She wanted to know why God would tell her to go places and when she would do what she was instructed she would encounter deeper and darker bondage with the devil. One time she said that God told her to go to the bowling alley in the middle of the night. When she got there, she said that some demons came running out the front door. This woman was so convinced that God was talking to her and putting her in a position of spiritual captivity that she started to get upset with God. I told her that it was not God, but Satan playing games with her to lead her into a deeper bondage. She rejected what I said and went on her way.

While there is no spiritual captivity caused by God. Some people are taken spiritually captive without a reason. If Satan's binding is without cause, God's glory will always shine in the deliverance that comes. When Jesus was out ministering there was a man that was blind. The disciples wanted to know how he ended up like this and asked who had sinned. They inquired on whether it was him or someone in his generations. John 9:3 says, *"Jesus answered, Neither hath this man sinned, nor his parents: but that the works of God should be made manifest in him."* Many mighty men and women of God have been birthed out of captive places. Some may refer to this as a desert experience. When Job of the bible had lost his children, his money, his health and the respect of his wife, many thought that he had brought these things on himself, but he had not. It was a place of testing for Job and testimony to the glory of God. The bible says that God blessed the latter days of Job more than the first.

When God releases you to be tried and tested of the devil, it always leads to a greater liberty. Also if you continuously reject the will of God he will release you into a reprobate mind. Romans 1:28 says, *"And even as they did not like to retain God in their knowledge, God gave them over to a reprobate mind, to do those things which are not convenient;"* Reprobate is a spiritual state that is cutoff from God. It is a captivity chosen by those who rebel against God.

While Satan can and will put people into a captive state. Most times spiritual captivity works hand in hand between the individual and the devil. It is most often the sinful mind and acts that carry a person in bondage. If people really knew the weight of their decisions in the spirit realm, they would not do most of the things they do. James 1:14 states, *"But every man is tempted, when he is drawn away of his own lust, and enticed. Then when lust hath conceived, it bringeth forth sin: and sin, when it is finished, bringeth forth death."* This place of spiritual death is where Satan rules. Luke 22:31-33 says, *"And the Lord said, Simon, Simon, behold, Satan hath desired to have you, that he may sift you as wheat: But I have prayed for thee, that thy faith fail not: and*

when thou art converted, strengthen thy brethren.
". Jesus understood the need to be strong and not captive in the spirit.

Satan's goal from the beginning has been to cut you off from God. It started in the Garden with Adam and Eve. It was a blessed place full of liberty and peace. Adam was given rule over the land and was allowed to enjoy the abundance of it. This access and abundance was cut short when he and Eve decided to sin against God. The bible says that death entered the world after Adams sin. Death is a place of captivity naturally and spiritually. It is the final resting place of Satan and all those that chose to follow him instead of God. Sin is the bridge to this state. Sin is the reason that Satan is no longer in heaven and sin will be the only reason why anyone will find themselves in eternal hell and death.

Season for the Flesh

When the time was approaching for Jesus to be betrayed and taken by the soldiers, he and some of his disciples were in the garden. Jesus was troubled because he knew that the time of his death was near. He asked the disciples to watch out with him while he prayed. When Jesus had finished praying, he found the disciples sound asleep. It must have been pretty disheartening for Jesus to find the ones closest to him sleeping while his torture and death were so near. Jesus said to them, *"What, could ye not watch with me one hour? Watch and pray, that ye enter not into temptation: the spirit indeed is willing, but the flesh is weak."* Matthew 26:40-41. After Jesus said this he went into prayer again and when he returned he found the disciples asleep again. The bible says that their eyes were "heavy".

This heaviness in the flesh that the disciples were experiencing is the same heaviness that plagues all of us. It is the weight of a sinful and unrepentant nature. In Romans 5:14 it says *"Nevertheless death reigned from Adam to Moses, even over them that had not sinned after the similitude of Adam's transgression, who is the figure of him that was to come."* This death reign is the result of original sin and the nature of the flesh. The flesh in God's eyes is an adversary and enemy to the will of God. God even stated in Genesis that his spirit would not always strive with man, because man was flesh.

Thousands of years later we now see why God made the statement he did about the flesh. The world has become a place where people strive to find personal pleasure that appeals to their flesh. This personal pleasure many times involves things that are adverse to God's word. The world has become more and more an accepting and inclusive society. A society that embraces you as long as you don't hurt someone else. But God is not just concerned about you hurting someone else, he is concerned about you hurting yourself through your willful rejection of his word.

The rejection of God's word and its requirements destroys your ability to have a liberated life. People may feel like doing what they want makes them free, but it is the end result that determines the reality of your decisions. The flesh is not your friend and will never be. The flesh lives to serve its desires and that's all. Its desires are not eternal so it seeks to enjoy itself while it's got a chance.

While we seek to live and make it through this life, our decisions on how we live this life are affected by many natural and spiritual sources. These sources can lead us in many different directions. Some of these influences are generational, peer influenced, heart conditioned, offense based, addiction based, and worldly acceptance motivated...many times running together to entangle a person in spiritual bondage.

Generational

Many times when ministering to people, I find that their problems are rooted in things of the past. When I dig deeper many times I find the same issues and life experiences happened in their parents or grandparents lives. These problems leap from generation to generation with no one ever finding a solution, often times resulting in a helpless embracing of the issue. Many know these issue as generational curses. Their origins can be one or two generations deep or can extend for multiple generations over. It is a spiritual oppression that can destroy families.
If a boy grows up seeing his mother beaten by his father, it becomes a natural part of his life. If the mother never leaves and continues to deal with it, he may assume that this is the order that's followed when men and women are married. When the young boy becomes an adult and decides to get married, he may start to treat his wife the same way he saw his father treat his mother. It is what is normal to him.

Although this may be obviously evil, this spiritual oppression on families will continue unless the reality and repentance from these sins are embraced.

When I was about to get married, I consulted with an older gentlemen I knew well. He told me that once I was married for about a year, I would start to have urges to have a mistress. I thought to myself, "that's crazy"....I hadn't seen my father cheat on my mother, so why would I do it to my wife. It was not normal or good and I had not seen it in my generations, so I was not influenced. He explained to me that he had seen it many times and it was ok.

Sometimes divorce and broken marriages can become generational in nature. When it is seen as an option and others around you have done it, the decision to divorce becomes a more ready solution to problems. Devils are good providing options. They will tell you anything and everything to get you to do something outside of the will of God. If they can get examples and influence through your family then all the better for their efforts to get you to embrace it.

As far as the list of generational bondages that can be passed down, the list is as long as the list of sin. From adultery to drug addiction, to depression and pride, a whole book could be written on this topic alone.

Being Unequally Yoked

Many of the bad habits people picked up in life are from time they spent with friends and associates. There are countless stories about people who seemed to be good people until they started hanging around a different crowd of people. I cannot tell you how many times I have heard the story about the good guy who is now in jail, on drugs, or dead because they got mixed in with the wrong crowd. Children tend to be very vulnerable to this because children are constantly growing and looking for understanding in their lives. Some children start off sweet and end up being very evil adults. Others start off being very difficult and disobedient but turn out to be great people.

Before I entered high school I never said a curse word, but as soon as all of my friends started cursing, it seemed like the normal thing to do. I made it apart of who I was and the only time I didn't curse was in the presence of my mother and out of earshot of anyone in church. By the time I made it to college every other word was dirty and I thought that was how people talked. When all the people around you are doing wrong and no one is listening to God, I guarantee that their are devils influencing conversations. If Satan knows you will listen to and take advice from someone who he has control of it makes it easier from him to bring you into a captive place.

Heart Conditioned

I always tell people that everything starts with the heart. We read in scripture that love is the foundation for everything we do with God. It doesn't matter how well you do anything else for God if you don't have love. A proper heart condition before God would be one that loves God first and makes its decisions based on that love. When this condition of love for God is not realized then we see many flow into bondage. The bible says in 1John 2:15, *"Love not the world, neither the things that are in the world. If any man love the world, the love of the Father is not in him."*

      The willful continuance of things that are sinful is a heart condition. Jesus said those that love him will follow his commands. Good hearts do righteous things and bad hearts do unrighteous things. Judas betrayed Jesus because he loved silver more than him. When you love something it can be a detriment to you if it is not from God. Our heart connection places the object of our affection at the top of the list in everything we do. If you love cars more than God, then everything you do will lead you back to the cars. If you love food more than God, then your focus will be the opportunity to eat. When we place things in our heart above God, we idolize these things. Idolizing things will only lead us to destruction.

Offense

      When I first started my ministry, one of the verses God gave me was the parable of the sower in the 13th chapter of Matthew. The thing that stood out to me was how out the four types of people that received the word of God in their life only one was able to produce fruit in their life. The others were lead away from God by loose connections to God, offense, and cares of the world. Those three things are some of the most effective ways Satan uses to dismantle your relationship with God. The word of God calls Satan the accuser of the brethren. He is the one that goes to one brother and tells him that the other is not really his friend and then turns around and goes to the other brother and says see I told you your brother didn't like you. If there is ever division and separation in the church, I guarantee that Satan is somewhere stirring up offense.

Offense opens the door to decisions that would not have been made unless the offense was present. When people commit to God, they often say they will never leave, but let them become angry with God or someone associated with him and they will leave.

Offense leads people away from God and it can manifest itself in many other ways. I cannot tell you how many times I have seen and heard of people killing one another because of minor offenses and disagreements. I recently saw a story of a man that killed his friend because he misunderstood a text he got from him.

Offense is one of those things that can change a person's entire life in a moment. All people encounter offense, but it is what you do with it that gives it power. Many times when people get offended they abruptly respond and do things that reflect and over reflect the offense was done to them. Offense can lead to captivity in many ways and can in itself be captivity. Some people get hurt as children and go through the rest of their life being offended. It can result in bitterness, anger, depression, murder, and many other types of sins. Sometimes people that were victims become the victimizers because of offense. I have heard of people who were molested as children end up molesting a child themselves when they become an adult. You might ask yourself; how can a victim end up on the other side of things? When a person is offended Satan comes in through offense and tries to add many things. This offense roots itself in un-forgiveness (ongoing offense) and creates bitterness in a person's heart. Bitterness is a place of offense that has been lodged in some ones heart for so long it has become rotten. Once it becomes lodged in your heart it becomes a strongman. This strongman opens the door to many other types of spirits to enter into your life. Spiritual strongmen are the gate keepers for spiritual captivity of individuals.

Many times marriages collapse because of ongoing offense. This offense opens the door to abuse, infidelity, jealousy, disrespect, depression, etc. Marriage is a powerful position in the spirit realm. Jesus recognized this power when he said in Matthew 18:19-20, *"Again I say unto you, That if two of you shall agree on earth as touching any thing that they shall ask, it shall be done for them of my Father which is in heaven. For where two or three are gathered together in my name, there am I in the midst of them."* Agreement in marriage brings great authority. Disagreement and offense in marriage brings destruction.

Addictions of Flesh

I used to work with a guy that smoked electronic cigarettes. He would sit and puff on that thing every day... all day long. I noticed that he would also look at pictures of different electronic cigarettes online. I asked him how he started smoking electronic cigarettes. He told me that he used to smoke regular cigarettes but he was trying to stop. I thought to myself he had only traded one addiction for another. Over time as I learned more about him I found out that he was also attending Alcoholics Anonymous meetings. It was apparent that he was jumping from one thing to another. The flesh will have you replacing one addiction for another. The true issue was not the alcohol or cigarettes, but the addictive nature of the flesh that wants relief. Addiction is a nasty place of captivity. Crack addicted mothers have sold their children for another high. Some alcoholics have drank rubbing alcohol for another high. Even in the more acceptable behaviors the entanglements of addiction can be devastating. Food can rule over people's lives and cause them to worship it. Sex outside of marriage can lead to disease, children out of wedlock, deadly soul ties, etc. The flesh is addiction prone and can often shift from one addiction to another based on what it is given access to.

  Sex addiction can become a spiritually devastating condition. Sex is a desire of the flesh that when out of control can leave a person helpless to the desires of it. If it is engaged in outside of a male & female marriage it can control a person's life. The bible says that once a person engages in sex outside of Christian marriage, that person sins against their own body and God. The entanglements of uncontrolled sex addiction opens the door for adultery, homosexual sex, and other deviant behavior.

Worldly Acceptance Motivated

  When God made the nation of Israel a chosen

people, he had a plan for how the people would govern themselves under him. He first gave them prophets, then he placed judges over the people. The nation grew and became mighty. As they increased in size, their heart started to change. They became adamant that they wanted a king. Unfortunately, they wanted to be like the rest of the world. They didn't understand that God was their king.

How many times have you heard of people starting out humble and as time went on and success started to increase they changed and completely went another direction. It's almost as if they feel they have arrived and now they want their seat in the world. The desire for worldly acceptance takes you out of position with God. You cannot be accepted by the world and God also. Jesus said in John 15:18-19, *"If the world hate you, ye know that it hated me before it hated you. If ye were of the world, the world would love his own: but because ye are not of the world, but I have chosen you out of the world, therefore the world hateth you."* The fear of rejection or loss of acceptance can lead you into a deeply captive place. We even see churches these days changing their doctrines to reflect what is most acceptable in society. In Revelations Jesus emphasized the need for some churches to go back to their first state, before they become so wealthy, influential, and mixed with world.

It is very dangerous for those who desire to be alive in the spirit to desire worldly acceptance because it requires compromise. Comprise causes the things of God to become lukewarm and inefficient. Once a person becomes lukewarm, they lose the power to resist the onslaught of Satan. The reason why we see such a quick change in Christian ideals in the world is because once a small tear is exploited it can quickly become a massive hole. This massive hole will allow things to come into a Christians life that they would have never embraced if they had not allowed compromise on smaller matters to happen.

Chapter 2
Reality of The Spirit Realm

1Peter 5:8 *"Be sober, be vigilant; because your adversary the devil, as a roaring lion, walketh about, seeking whom he may devour:"*

When I decided to change my life and live for Jesus Christ, things changed. I had finally made up my mind that I would live for Jesus. I was nervous but encouraged that the rest of my life would be easy because of my decision. I immediately went out and began to discuss how Jesus had changed my life with people expecting to get a positive response. I was surprised at what people would say to me. Some would tell me I was too young, some told me I was going to mess up my dating life, and others said that I was lying. They said I would eventually go back to being the same person I was previously. As I took all the criticism and continued on my journey, things became a lot stranger. After about a month of being a new Christian I found myself ministering to a young lady on the phone. I asked her if I could pray with her. When I started to pray I started hearing growling noises on the phone and they became louder and louder. It made me so nervous that I stopped praying for her. She didn't notice anything. A month or so later I was ministering to a young man at my job, when a coworker interrupted our conversation and began to curse me out. He was spitting all over the place. He was extremely angry that I was talking about Jesus. It really caught me off guard considering that this same man had always been nice to me and spoke highly of me.

  As time when on in my Christian walk I noticed that where ever I was there was a lot of trouble. It seemed that around every corner there was a lot of pressure and affliction. During this first year of living for Jesus, I found myself racing home every day to pray because the day had been so difficult. I was crying out to God on a daily basis. During these prayer sessions I would always ask God why I was going through so much.

  One day while I was working I decided to search on having issues as a Christian. I found a website on spiritual warfare. It was as if someone had given me a new lease of life. Every frustration, every disappointment, every offense, began to make sense. I realized that I was a Christian who loved God, but there is an adversary that I had to be aware of. 1Peter 5:8 says *"Be sober, be vigilant; because your adversary the devil, as a roaring lion, walketh about, seeking whom he may devour:"* I had been a Christian for a whole year but had not given thought to Satan looking to afflict me and my need to resist evil.

The media, especially television and the movies are good at making evil look harmless. We see shows on witchcraft, devils, sexual immorality and all manner of evil. It's at people's finger tips and people are constantly ingesting and glorifying evil on the big screen. Even reality shows are popping up celebrating evil and people doing things that are in no way holy and pure. The demonic is paraded as some type of fantasy that people can watch but in some way it doesn't affect them.

Devils are real and the influence they have on people's lives is catastrophic. Many look to natural causes and effects regarding things affect their lives. They hardly ever realize that there is another realm that is contending for your soul. When strange or odd things happens it gets dismissed or written off to chance. In the grand scheme of things the spirit realm is counted as something for folklore and distant fables.

Ultimately Satan's plan is at work making people forget that he exists and focusing on the seen versus the unseen. Satan wants you to think that everything starts and stops with your own wants and desires and that if you position yourself correctly you can have all of your desires and live that life that you want. He is the master of stirring up pride in a person. This was the same sin that caused him to fall from Heaven. Isaiah 14:12-15 says *"How art thou fallen from heaven, O Lucifer, son of the morning! how art thou cut down to the ground, which didst weaken the nations! For thou hast said in thine heart, I will ascend into heaven, I will exalt my throne above the stars of God: I will sit also upon the mount of the congregation, in the sides of the north: I will ascend above the heights of the clouds; I will be like the most High. Yet thou shalt be brought down to hell, to the sides of the pit."*

  Just like the devil is all about himself, he wants you to be all about yourself. A prideful heart opens the door to a selfish heart. I have heard some professing Satanists say that they don't believe in the devil. They say they just want to do what they want and not have to submit to a higher power. I know most people would never say they were devil worshippers, but many don't know that allowing sinful things to control their life is in essence following Satan. In scripture he is called disobedience and those that go against the will of God are called the children of disobedience. Being disobedient to God is a great way to cut off the redeeming power of God from your life.

  Many people find themselves afflicted by evil spirits because they will not submit to God. The bible says that deliverance is the children's bread, meaning that the spirit of God sets free those that are the children of God. If you are not a child of God, you are in many ways subject to the power of Satan. The bible even says to be outside of God's covering is to also be against your own self. When God gives instruction to his ministers to teach people who are not under his covering he says in 2 Timothy 2:25-26 *"In meekness instructing those that oppose themselves; if God peradventure will give them repentance to the acknowledging of the truth; And that they may recover themselves out of the snare of the devil, who are taken captive by him at his will."* To live in this life without a relationship with Jesus leaves you open to being taken captive by the will of Satan.

    Captivity in the spirit is not always a negative experience from a natural or worldly perspective. For instance, when people have sex outside of marriage they sin against God and open themselves up to the power of Satan. However, in many circles, sex before marriage is natural and just something that people do. I know before I got saved I very rarely heard anyone talking about waiting until they got married to have sex. The only time I would hear it was in a few church services. This is the ploy of Satan. He wants to normalize sin and have you enter his domain unaware. What better way to take people captive than to enslave them and have them thinking that they are free and can do what they want.

    Hidden oppression and redirected focuses are the reality of the spirit realm. Some would call it smoke and mirrors, meaning that what you see and feel is not necessarily what is. To make a judgement of wellbeing or goodness based on personal reality limits a person to human experience. The bible says that God is a spirit and that he created the world. So it can be said that the natural world is a manifestation of the spirit. To only live on one side only gives you a halfway perception.

    Many times when things happen on the news there is a rush to judgement and people form their own opinions based on what information they had. As time goes on we often find out that there is more to the story. Once all the facts are in then there is usually a change in the feelings of people who made judgements from the beginning. People living their lives outside of the reality of the spirit is the same way. They live a life according to their desires and they make judgements according to what seems right to them. They live and die at the beat of their own drum not understanding that there is another reality that provides the sticks and the drum.

In the book of Numbers, the king of the Moabites was concerned because the Israelites were becoming numerous and powerful. He sent his servants to ask the Prophet Balaam for help. They asked him to curse the Israelites so that they could defeat them. God told Balaam to not go with the men and the king and to not curse the Israelites because they were blessed. After a few tries and promises, Balaam was insistent that he personally wouldn't go against what God said pertaining to Israel. He asked them to provide him a house full of silver and gold and he would talk to God again. This time God being upset told him to go with the men and say what he told him. After Balaam saddled up his donkey and began on his journey an angel of the lord with a sword stood in his way. The donkey seeing the angel became scared and tried to turn into a field. Balaam got upset with the donkey and began to whip it because he could not see the angel. Balaam tried to turn the donkey in another direction, but the angel blocked that way also. The donkey being scared fell against a wall and crushed Balaam's foot. Balaam hit the donkey again not seeing the angel. Then the donkey just gave up and fell under Balaam. Balaam was so frustrated that he began to beat the donkey. The donkey spoke to Balaam and asked him why he was hitting him. Immediately the angel of the lord appeared to Balaam. He seeing the angel with the sword, bowed his head and fell on his face. The angel told him that his way was perverse and he was there to stop him. The donkey had saved his life by getting out of the way.

    This story of Balaam is very familiar to how people are affected by the spirit realm. They are affected by it but don't have a clue until it is revealed to them. In the case of Balaam he had some connection with God, but still did not have a full revelation of what was going on in the spirit. How much worse is it for someone who is completely disconnected from the Spirit of God. People make decisions based on their circumstances and own desires. When Balaam's donkey was acting up he immediately assumed that there was a problem with the donkey, so he whipped the donkey to get a desired reaction. The reaction he got didn't make sense to him because he didn't have a full understanding on what was going on around him and was making decisions on limited knowledge. The more he fought with the donkey the more entangled he became, ultimately causing a lot of harm for him and donkey.

    When we do not follow the will of God, we can experience trouble in the natural and in the spirit. When you are in the will of God, you are able to navigate the spiritual and the natural. While good and bad people may go through things in this natural life, when you are following the direction of God, you will always find liberty in the spirit.

There was a movie that came out several years ago. It was called "They Live". It is a story about a man that stumbled across a box of sunglasses that when put on revealed the true identity of people pretending to be humans. The sunglasses also revealed the true messages behind the billboards, tv commercials, and magazines. The glasses showed a completely different reality than the one everybody had embraced. All the people that were in positions of authority and wealth were mainly the false humans. Nobody had a clue what was going on except the ones deceiving and the ones that had their eyes open with the sunglasses. The man who had the sunglasses was able to navigate his way around the deceivers and so he was not subject to the traps and manipulation that others were. This insight he had gave him the ability to get an advantage over the deceivers.

When you have a true revelation of the unseen, it no longer has as an advantage of deception. It can no longer redirect focus and misplace aggression. It weakens its effectiveness and opens the door for it to be conquered. You cannot beat an adversary unless you know that it exists.

Many great armies have suffered huge casualties against weaker opponents because they had the element of surprise. Some call it guerilla warfare. It is where the opponent has become a master at hiding under cover, in the dark of the night, and amongst the civilian population. Friendly innocents during the day can become deadly opponents at night.

Many things that have an appearance of harmlessness and innocence in our lives in reality will bring spiritual oppression and misery to our lives. This is why it is so important to live according to the word of God. There is no deception in Jesus Christ. A relationship with him only gets better and better. To know Jesus is to have full revelation and direction as we travel on the natural and spiritual journey through this life.

    It has been said that the biggest trick that Satan has played on mankind is to make them think that he doesn't exist. I met a minister many years ago that told me he had not mentioned the devil in church in the last several years. He was very proud that he had removed any mention of Satan and knew to the date that he stopped speaking of him. As childrren of God, we have to be careful, because until Christ returns we have an adversary to resist. I can pretend that there is no crime in the city I live in, but it doesn't mean I won't be a victim of crime. If a person is more aware of their surroundings when things happen they are more prepared. Ignorance and having a false sense of security only leads us into captivity. Jesus said in John 16:33 *"These things I have spoken unto you, that in me ye might have peace. In the world ye shall have tribulation: but be of good cheer; I have overcome the world."*

    Ignorance only leads people to a bad place. To pretend like something is not there only makes them more of a helpless victim when the thing they ignored attacks. I remember a pastor that called me for deliverance. He had been stricken with multiple health afflictions in the middle of his ministry. He had been to several doctors and no one could figure out why he was sick. After speaking with him for a little while, I asked him had he dealt with demons. He told me that when he would pray for people sometimes they would start to show demonic activity. He said that when that would happen he would stop praying for them. At that moment I knew the issue that he had. He was preaching but was afraid of demons and tried to pretend like they didn't exist.

      God has called us to be soldiers for his kingdom. The bible says in Exodus 15:3 that *"The LORD is a man of war: the LORD is his name."* meaning that God operates by force. We as his children are to be at war against the works of the devil. 2Timothy 2:4 *"No man that warreth entangleth himself with the affairs of this life; that he may please him who hath chosen him to be a soldier."* Those that are Christ's are chosen to resist evil and win souls for him until his return. This life is a preparation for eternal life. We live in this world as strangers in a foreign land knowing that we are citizens of heaven.

Chapter 3
Improper Births

2Corinthians 11:3-4 *"But I fear, lest by any means, as the serpent beguiled Eve through his subtilty, so your minds should be corrupted from the simplicity that is in Christ. For if he that cometh preacheth another Jesus, whom we have not preached, or if ye receive another spirit, which ye have not received, or another gospel, which ye have not accepted, ye might well bear with him."*

When Adam sinned in the garden, they disconnected everyone born after them from God. We understand in scripture that when God created Adam he created him after his likeness, but after Adam sinned, his offspring were created in the likeness of Adam. This likeness of Adam is the reason why we need Jesus.

When we receive Jesus as our lord and savior and turn from our sins, we become born again. We are born into the spirit with Jesus Christ.

Satan tempted Adam and Eve and caused them to be cut off from God, But God gave his son Jesus to redeem mankind back into a relationship with him. After Satan saw that the work he had done in Adam was being overcome he began trying to defile the relationship a person has with Jesus Christ. Satan understands the benefit of being connected to God. He was once connected himself. He wants to destroy everyone's relationship with God like he did his own.

Every time a soul gets saved the angels in heaven rejoice and the workers of darkness are defeated. This battle in life is ultimately for souls. Being a battle there are strategies for victory on each side. One of the devils largest tools is defilement. Defilement in spiritual terms means to be unclean and unholy before God.

Everything that comes before God must be holy and pure. When the Levite high priest for the nation of Israel would enter into the presence of God in his holy temple, he had to be pure. The priest couldn't even have a blemish on his clothing. Before the priest would enter in the innermost room were the spirit of God was, the sanctuary attendants would tie a rope to his leg and put bells on him. After he entered in they would listen at the entrance. If the bells stopped ringing they knew that the priest had died and they would drag him out of the room. The requirement to be pure exposes the need for a mediator that can cover and purify our impurity. This mediator is Jesus Christ.

The Levite priesthood with all its holy men, traditions, and sacrifices were never sufficient to God. God needed a perfect priest that was pure that would serve as a sacrifice also. When Jesus rose from the grave he became our high priest forever. It says in Hebrews 5:9-10 *"And being made perfect, he became the author of eternal salvation unto all them that obey him; Called of God an high priest after the order of Melchisedec."* His perfection allows him to be the perfect mediator without spot or blemish. The bible says that he sits on the right hand of God making intercession for us. What the human priest couldn't do, Jesus does. He is the only way that we may remain pure before God.

The devil works tirelessly to stop our relationship with Jesus. His strategy is to cause you to have a defiled or unpure connection with God. This connection can take form in a number of different ways.

Some of these ways include:

- False salvation experience
- Carnal Christianity
- Hearing from the spirit realm but not from God
- Not being mature in spirit before you lead others
- Taking on the wrong purpose and position in Church

False Salvation Experience

Everyone knows that when you build a house that the foundation is extremely important. It is the beginning of everything that is built on it. The way you start usually guides you to the finish. When a house is built on a bad foundation it causes structural problems for everything on top of it. In order to fix everything else the foundation must be reset. Many years ago I was appraising a house for its value and after I had looked the house over I noticed that there was a large hole in the foundation. This hole destroyed the value of the house because it was not safely habitable without it being repaired.

    The bible says that without Jesus there is no connection with God. Jesus has to be our lord and savior to receive eternal salvation. He is the rock and the foundation of our faith. The revelation of needing a savior, repenting, receiving Jesus as him is a delicate and precious time for the believer. It is the foundation of our relationship with God and the most essential part of receiving eternal salvation.

    The time of our confession and salvation in Jesus Christ is not based on a fleshly feeling. It is based on an inner commitment in the soul. It is a place of transition that carries us from the old sinful nature to a redeemed spiritual nature.

    If a person misunderstands what it means to be saved then they will live their life with a false salvation assurance. To just believe in Jesus is not enough. You must believe that he died on the cross and rose from the grave for your sins. Once you have made this confession you must live to obey him. Matthew 7:21, *"Not every one that saith unto me, Lord, Lord, shall enter into the kingdom of heaven; but he that doeth the will of my Father which is in heaven."* If we say we are followers of Jesus Christ then we will exhibit it in our actions. In a false salvation experience there is not a hearts conviction of sin or the revelation of the need for a savior. The result of this is usually continued sin and an insecure Christian worldview.

Carnal Christianity

One thing I was taught in life is to do what you say and say what you do. There is an honor in keeping your word and also living by the things that you profess. God wants his people to not only say they love him, but show it in their everyday lives. He even desires that we love him so much that we first seek to do his will first. Jesus summed it up when he said in John 14:23-24 *"If a man love me, he will keep my words: and my Father will love him, and we will come unto him, and make our abode with him. He that loveth me not keepeth not my sayings: and the word which ye hear is not mine, but the Father's which sent me."* Jesus was trying to be clear that to say one thing but do another is not acceptable in Gods eyes. If we say we love Jesus we should do what he says we should do. Unfortunately, many Christian circles are starting to do differently than what God would have them to do.

Growing up in church, the preachers would always be talking about living right and serving the lord. Most sermons turned you away from yourself and directed you to Jesus. When you were in church you knew it and if someone wasn't living right it was a big deal, because people understood that being a Christian meant you were expected to have a righteous standard for your life.

These days I have seen many ministries popping up that don't teach holy living and staying away from sin. They teach more of a selfish type message focused on personal attainment and self-gratification. They stay away from telling people to repent of their sins and focus more on being a morally good person. They make church exciting with gimmicks, they bring in secular artists to do praise and worship, they avoid subjects that are controversial like homosexuality and preach a word that can be accepted by all. They allow people who are filled with sin to hold positions in churches and turn a blind eye to a pastors with dark secrets. It's the modern day carnal church. Jesus said it well when he called many of the spiritual leaders of his day, "hypocrites".

I know of a minister that was sleeping with many of the women in his church. He sought direction from a minister friend because he was confused. He couldn't understand why when he preached people would fall out and he would move in great power, but he was addicted to sex and continuously slept around. It had been going on for over a decade. It was obvious what was going on spiritually in this situation. Satan had high jacked his ministry many years ago and replaced the power of the Holy Spirit, with a demonic anointing. He was captive to a demonic spirit but didn't know. He thought that since people were falling out and he had a level of power, that God was still using him. This is how people become entangled in being a carnal Christian. They are cut off from the things of God, but don't know it. Many continuously sin and think because nothing bad is happening to them in the natural that they are ok. They don't understanding that they are captive and deceased in the spirit.

 Big crowds, cool preachers, professional musicians, and large budgets are not a sign of the move of God. Carnal people look at natural success and popularity, but God judges the heart of a man. Our hearts foundation is love for Jesus and the desire to do his will. The outward expression of our love for Jesus will produce spiritual fruit in our own lives and in the lives of others. Carnal Christians don't look for fruit, they look for power, prestige, and present circumstances. It is the same thing that the world goes after. When churches preach carnality as good thing, their membership sky rockets because the people want to be rich, powerful, and have all that they want right now, especially when they can keep sinning and still get it. It is a false righteousness and defiled relationship with God.

 I was in a church service one time and the preacher asked, "where are all my God made millionaires". The crowds of people that were in the church began to scream and shout. They were excited and motivated to get financially rich for Jesus. I asked the lord about this and he told me that they were, "spoiled children". I personally believe God wants to make you rich, but its not as much in the natural as it is in the spirit. Carnal Christians think that natural wealth is the inheritance of the saints. Natural riches pass away, but spiritual riches last an eternity.

 I have heard many people talk about how God has blessed them, but are not really focused on living for God. Just because a person has a lot of money doesn't mean that God has blessed them. Satan would love to give you things and convince you that staying the way you are is ok. He wants you full of sin, riding in a luxury car saying that God is blessing you. It is that captive place that warps the reality of the spirit and convinces people who are dead in the spirit that they are alive.

Who's Voice Did You Hear?

When we are in prayer there are three different things that can communicate with us. They are our own thoughts, words from demons, and words from God. Knowing the difference can lead you to spiritual freedom and not knowing the difference will certainly lead you into bondage. Hearing clearly from the lord takes prayer, patience, and a solid relationship. It is not something you just freely do at your leisure without a relationship with him. Your spiritual ear has to be developed that you may be able to hear clearly.

In many years of ministering I encountered many that say they hear from God. I believe that many do, but there were many that did not. One of the worst ways to be captive to demons is to think they are God speaking to you. The word they speak will lead you into to a false assurance of Gods approval, false power, false purpose, and worst of all influence others with the false words from them. False words to others can cause wounds that last a lifetime.

If you are in sin and not living by the word of God, more than likely God is not having casual conversations with you. God is a holy God and the bible specifically says that repentance is necessary before a regular communication can be established with him. When you have commited your life to Jesus and live by his word, then a clear line of communication can be established with him.

<u>Spiritual babies having babies</u>

In recent years there has been an epidemic of teenagers having babies. It is really sad because teenagers usually are not that good at taking care of themselves, much less taking care of a young child. Many times the teenager's parents or grandparents end up having to raise the babies because the teenager is not mature enough to take care of all the baby's needs. I have even heard stories of girls getting pregnant because all their friends were pregnant and they didn't want to be left out. What state of mind are these young people in when they bring children into the world without having a clue to life? Babies raising babies can cause suffering for generations. These same issues are prevalent in the spirit realm also. There is a difference between an adult and a child. There is a difference between the mature and the immature. Those that are mature do things differently than those that are immature. Adults make different decisions than children do. When you are mature in the spirit your decision making process is different than when you are a babe. Mature people in the spirit have different responsibilities in spirit than those who are babes. Leading the people of God is for the mature in spirit. The bible says in Hebrews 5:13-14 *"For every one that useth milk is unskilful in the word of righteousness: for he is a babe. But strong meat belongeth to them that are of full age, even those who by reason of use have their senses exercised to discern both good and evil."* People acquire a lot knowledge in today's church environments. With the internet coming to its maturity and people putting things online at a fast pace, it is amazing to me how information travels at such a rapid pace now. Just because information is available doesn't mean it should be obtained. If someone is not mature in the spirit, they should stay away from the mature things until they are mature. When a person is immature in the spirit they are not prepared to wrestle with the things that come with operating in maturity. For instance, if a person tries to operate as a prophet before they are mature, they are subject to being deceived and operating in the wrong spirit. Christian babes can sometimes develop a form of power but their immaturity is exposed because they cannot overcome sin and walk in the simple things like humility and love.

     Jesus spoke is his word about the blind leading the blind. He said that if people that are blind follow people that are blind they will fall into a ditch together. To put it in spiritual context…if someone cannot see into the spirit, they cannot lead you in the things of the spirit. Unfortunately people who are blind in the spirit can't tell who is and who isn't blind. That's why it can be so difficult. When a person first starts on a spiritual journey, whoever assists them in the beginning is usually the person they continue to follow. No matter if it is right or wrong they will follow them because the trust is established from the beginning. I cannot tell you how many times I have met someone who has or is following someone who is blind in the spirit. Ultimately you find out they follow the person for other reasons outside of their spiritual leadership. Sometimes when they really follow them for what they can learn in the spirit, buy they usually end up being lead into confusion and abused in other areas of the relationship with the person.

Some people live their whole lives living a spiritual lie. They think they have the truth but are living a deceived life. Sometimes the leaders are babies in the spirit and are not strong enough to lead anyone, but they take the position of leader because it is available to them. Its not that God has ordained them for the position of leadership, but they through their own will or someone else's will are placed in a position of authority. God puts his leaders in place, not men. It is how King David was able to become king, and how the son of a carpenter came to save mankind.

Captive Leaders

In many circles people follow their leaders every word. No matter if they follow the word of God or not. They become broken records for bad doctrine and never learn the truth. If the leader is weak in an area, they cause every one that follows them to be weak in that area. If it is bad doctrine, then they create a group with bad doctrine. If they have trouble with sin, they create a group of people who have trouble with sin. If they love material items, they create a group of people who love material items with them. Its what babies do. They create a reality around them that satisfies their needs and understandings. Just as Adam had children after his own likeness because of his sin, so also leaders who are a spiritual babies, create spiritual children after their own likeness. They are babies having spiritual babies. You can only be as strong as the person you follow, it they are a babe then you certainly are.

    I had a dream a while ago that I was standing in a long line to visit a church. It was night time and the line was so long it stretched out into the street. As my young son and I approached the front door I peeked into the building and saw a coffin on the inside. I was shocked because I thought we were attending a church service. I looked over at the seats for service and no one was sitting. The seats were empty and people were just stopping by to look at the body. As I walked into the building the body in the casket started to move. Its arms were wailing in the air and it started to flip over and over. The deacons of the church came and tried to get the body to settle down. I asked if it was the pastor and they said that it was the pastor's son. I asked the lord why I was attending a funeral I thought was a church service. He showed me that people are attending churches where the spirit of God has departed and spiritually dead men are the main attraction. I asked him why the dead body was moving around. He said that sometimes bodies move before the rigor sets in. He showed me that dead things can appear to have life but only for a season. I asked him why it was the preacher's son. He showed me that it was generational problem. Leaders were creating people just like themselves who were absent of the spirit of God.

Hurt Births Hurt

One of the worst way people can become afflicted in the spirit realm is getting hurt by someone who was hurt. When people operate out of their hurt they do things to protect themselves and usually hurt others. It is a device that Satan uses over and over again to afflict people who follow people who never got free from their affliction. Whole ministries have been formed out of hurt and offence. To minister or lead people based on hurt is to be in the flesh. One time I had a minister call me wanting to start a church. I asked him why he felt the need to start a church. He said that he didn't agree with how the church he was attending handled some things. He said that they had not done anything sinful, he just thought he could do a better job. That wasn't a good reason and I told him he should let God tell him when to start a church.

When a person makes a decision out of hurt or disagreement, they are not listening to God. God is not the director of their decisions. Their emotions are in control. Emotions are personal feelings that should not be trusted when making decisions of a spiritual nature. Personal feelings can blind a person to God's will. Rather than allowing feelings to direct things, it is best to always look to God for direction in a situation. If a person is hurt and still dealing with the offense of a situation, they should seek to become fully healed before they try to lead others.

Who's laid their hands on you?

Paul was clear in the book of Timothy about not laying hands on people without the direction of the lord. It says in 1Timothy 5:22 *"Lay hands suddenly on no man, neither be partaker of other men's sins: keep thyself pure."* It should also be said that people should not allow people to place their hands on them and pray for them without knowing that they are strong spiritually.

When I was very new in the things of the spirit, I was attending a church that liked to do everything as a large corporate body. The pastor said over the loud speaker that we all had the power to cast out devils and that we should be laying our hands on people and praying for them. He asked that anyone who was dealing with depression to stand up. Several people throughout the sanctuary stood up. He instructed the rest of the church to get up and go over and pray for the depressed people. Me being sure of having the authority quickly headed over to pray for a man standing close by. I laid my hand on his shoulder along with several other people and we prayed for him. I felt good and was confident that I was operating in the power of God. The next day I found myself in a state of depression. Many depressed thoughts flowed through my mind and I was miserable for the next couple of days. After a couple of days of being down and out, I started to wonder why I was so depressed. I remembered that I had laid hands on the man that was depressed in the service. I had taken on the spirit he was wrestling with and was not strong enough to fight it off.

Even today, I always check with the spirit of God about laying hands on people, because you always have to keep in mind that its Gods power not your own. You use it at his discretion not your own. While the spiritually wise can discern when to and when not to lay hands on people, those who need hands laid on them many times cannot tell who to allow to pray for them and who to avoid. Before I became a leader in ministry, I didn't just allow people to lay hands on me. No matter how much I tried to be discerning I found that people would still try to call me up even if I didn't want them to. I was at a conference onetime and the speaker was extremely foolish and was doing crazy things during service. Before we could get out of the church, he tried to call all the youth up to pray for them. I would not let my children participate.

When someone has evil spirits in them, they can transfer the spirits in them by a simple touch of their hand. Spiritually when a person lays hands on a person and prays for them, either things flow from the person praying into the person they are praying for or the person being prayed for releases things into the person praying for them. Weather these things are good or bad depends on the spiritual makeup of the person praying and the person being prayed for. If the person praying for you has spiritual issues, when they lay hands on you and pray for you, you will probably contend with those same issues.

Wrong purpose and position

When I was growing up, the Pastor of the church was always seen as being holy and someone to go to when you needed direction. They were the attendants of the church and leaders of the church. During service they would sit facing the congregation in the pulpit. They were set apart to lead the flock. If anyone ever felt called by God, their most likely track would be to start to preach and eventually pastor a church. This cycle fostered the creation of many churches over the years. Many times these churches would have the same format, a main holy man and everyone else was a member.

While pastors are essential in leading and walking with a congregation, there are many other functions that are just as important positions in the Lord's church. The Apostle Paul said in 1 Corinthians 12:12-14 that *"For as the body is one, and hath many members, and all the members of that one body, being many, are one body: so also is Christ. For by one Spirit are we all baptized into one body, whether we be Jews or Gentiles, whether we be bond or free; and have been all made to drink into one Spirit. For the body is not one member, but many."* Paul relates the Body of Christ which is the church to the natural body. As a natural body functions as one, also the spiritual body functions as one. With any functioning body there are many parts that work together to make the body work. Every body part is needed so that the body can function properly. While there are some parts of our body that we find more attractive and more useful, I am sure that it would be hard to find anyone willing to give up any part of their body. Every part has a function that is useful. God's church works in the same way. While God's church is one, there are many people that are a part of it. These people are not just segregated into pastor and member, but there are many assignments and works in the body of Christ. Every assignment and position is needed so that church may be spiritually healthy.

    Knowing who you are and what you are supposed to do is key in living a free and fulfilled life. There are many people who are Christians, but are searching for their purpose as Christians. Not knowing who they are, many grasp onto the traditional lines of ministry leadership and often times find themselves unfilled and wandering in ministry. There are people who lead churches who were never meant to lead churches and people who have great talents to bless the church, but are never used because their gift to the church is not understood. Having a mature understanding of the word is not the only qualifier to start your own church. Speaking good and getting people excited is not a sign that God has cosigned on your ministry. These two things often times propel people to receive or take headship over a church.

    One of the most destructive tactics Satan uses to attack God's church and his people is having people misunderstand who they are. He wants to defile purpose to a place where the church doesn't function well. He tries to tell the foot it needs to be the hand and tells the thumb it needs to be the knee cap. This confusion creates a body that cannot function well, or function at all. God has called the church to function as it has been assigned. He gives us a group of 5 leadership gifts whose job is to bring the church into perfect alignment with Christ. In Ephesians 4:11-12 it says, *"And he gave some, apostles; and some, prophets; and some, evangelists; and some, pastors and teachers; For the perfecting of the saints, for the work of the ministry, for the edifying of the body of Christ:"* These five leadership gifts are many times rolled into the pastor role. The issue is that you cannot role all these gifts into one title. Each one of these roles has a separate place in the church. (1 Corinthians 12:27-29)

     If the leaders don't understand their roles and assignments, how can they help anyone else. Once leaders understand their role they can more easily direct or redirect people into the vocation that they have in the church. Every member knowing their role in the body of Christ solidifies the churches identity so that they can work together in unity.

Chapter 4
The Children's Bread

John 8:36 If the Son therefore shall make you free, ye shall be free indeed.

Houses Swept Clean

Before I got saved, I struggled to read the bible. Every time I would sit down to read I became distracted. The words would confuse me. It seemed as if it was just an old book with a lot of words that I couldn't understand. I thought that the bible was just confusing and boring and did not think that there was anything extra the bible could offer me. Every time I would try to read it I would become tired and sleepy. I would also find myself drifting into other thoughts at random.

    This struggle came to a dramatic end when I settled on living for Jesus Christ. As soon as I made my mind up to live according to God's will, reading the bible was no longer difficult. It was as if I had become a different person. I went from years and years of no reading to being able to sit for any length of time reading the word of God. I got to the point of spending endless nights reading and absorbing everything that the bible had to say. I felt like someone had just turned the lights on and I could see. Every struggle and misunderstanding I had with the word of God went away and I found myself able to understand and live by the word of God. When I look back at the shift in my ability to read the word, I realize that the reason I couldn't grasp the word of God, was because I was not delivered out of my old nature and my mind had not been renewed to the full revelation of Jesus Christ. There was an obvious new liberty that I had. This freedom had not been there before. I had been a person who could never stay focused, but suddenly I had absolute focus when it came to God's word.

    Not only did I get immediate freedom from not being able to read the word. Everything about me changed. I had been a person that cursed in almost every word that I spoke, but when I began my walk with Jesus Christ, even the words that came out of my mouth changed. I didn't have to pray to stop cursing, it just stopped. It wasn't even a struggle. My mind was completely renewed and transformed. God had done a complete work in my mind.

    The bible says that we are transformed by

the renewing of our minds. This renewal is a very important work that the Holy Spirit does to begin the cleansing process in our lives. God needs his people to be holy and pure and it is through the power of the Holy Spirit that we are able to break free from sin and spiritual oppression.

    I have talked to many people that were being oppressed by the devil and entangled in sin. Some were liberated immediately and some never got free. I have no doubt that the power of God could liberate any one of them, however many that desire deliverance never get it, because they lack one thing. This one thing is the willingness to be obedient to the spirit of God. Often they would call desperately wanting to be healed, but when I would start to minister to them they didn't want me to teach them, they didn't want a clearer understanding, they just wanted a prayer to send the affliction away. The ones that would listen, learn, and be obedient would always be blessed.

    Onetime a man called me for healing from overseas. He told me he had an affliction in his body that had been lasting for years. I prayed and immediately the spirit of God told me to tell him to go get a bottle of olive oil and anoint himself. With joy he got off the phone to leave for the store. Within five minutes he called me back and said that right after he left to go get oil, the pain went away. The spirit of God showed me that it wasn't the oil that was going to heal him but that he had the faith to go get the oil and do as God instructed him.

    It is always God's desire that we become free. As long as we are his children, spiritual liberty is always available to us. It is many times the lack of faith in Jesus Christ and his will that keeps people from being free. Jesus even encountered people during his time on earth that did not get healed by his power although it was available to them. When Jesus went into his own country the bible says in Mark 6:5-6 *"And he could there do no mighty work, save that he laid his hands upon a few sick folk, and healed them. And he marvelled because of their unbelief. And he went round about the villages, teaching."*

If you want to be spiritually free you have to believe that liberty is possible and that it is available to you. Jesus Christ's delivering power is activated by the faith of the believer. Many times when Jesus would heal people, he would tell them that it was their faith that loosed them from their bondage.

One day Jesus was walking in a city and a there was a woman nearby who had a blood disease. She had suffered this disease for twelve long years. The bible said that she had spent all her money on doctors but no one could heal her. When she saw Jesus, she worked her way to get near him and touched the border of his garment. After she touched him, Jesus felt some of the healing power in him leave his body and go into hers. Immediate Jesus told her in Luke 8:48, *"Daughter, be of good comfort: thy faith hath made thee whole; go in peace."* This healing happend because she dared to believe and put her faith in action. I believe her action of touching his garment was a move of faith that got her healed.

When Jesus was leaving out of the city of Jericho, there was a man sitting by the roadside. The bible refers to him as "blind Bartimaeus". When he heard that Jesus was passing by, he cried out begging that Jesus have mercy on him. When the people told him to quiet down, he cried even louder. Jesus heard his cries and told him to come to him. After Jesus spoke to him, Bartimaeus threw off his garment and went to Jesus. Jesus healed him of his blindness and told him, it was his faith that made him whole. He called on Jesus in his hour of despair and Jesus was faithful to heal him. This is our inheritance as the saints of God...that we may call on the name of Jesus and be saved.

      Jesus is the deliverer that came to set the captives free. This liberty was not only for physical or fleshly ailments, but also that we may be spiritually healed. When Jesus would tell people they were made whole, he was referring to them being physically and spiritually whole. This wholeness made them pure and swept clean from all bondages. By his stripes we are healed and set free. He died on the cross so that through his resurrection we may walk in the newness of life. This new life encompasses a purity of soul, body and spirit. It says in 1 Thessalonians 5:23, *"And the very God of peace sanctify you wholly; and I pray God your whole spirit and soul and body be preserved blameless unto the coming of our Lord Jesus Christ."* Basically meaning that every part of your being should be cleansed.

      Being made whole, you become a vessel that is clean and uncorrupted. Your uncorrupted vessel is made to be filled with the Spirit of God. When Paul wrote a letter to Timothy about staying away from sin and people keeping their vessels clean, He said, *"If a man therefore purge himself from these, he shall be a vessel unto honour, sanctified, and meet for the master's use, and prepared unto every good work."* 2Timothy 2:21. God cannot use us as Christians unless we have become prepared for his use.

One of Satan's primary tactics is to try and corrupt those who have become liberated in Christ. He wants to take the vessels and fill them with sin so that God cannot use them. Jesus said that when a spirit goes out a man it travels into dry places not being able to find rest. After a while it says that it will return to the place it was kicked out of. When it returns to the empty vessel it finds that it has been emptied, swept, and garnished. After finding the vessel empty it goes out and gets seven more spirits worse than it is and they enter in and dwell there. The person who was cleaned ends up worse off than they were to begin with.

One of the biggest keys to deliverance is that you must make it a lifestyle. This means that you allow the spirit of God to fill you up and you use it to maintain a righteous lifestyle. The Psalm of David prophetically spoke to this power that fills and maintains. It says in Psalms 23:5-6 *"Thou preparest a table before me in the presence of mine enemies: thou anointest my head with oil; my cup runneth over. Surely goodness and mercy shall follow me all the days of my life: and I will dwell in the house of the LORD for ever. "* The oil represents the setting apart accomplished through our connection with Christ. The cup running over is the fullness of the Holy Spirit. By being set apart and filled, Christians are able to walk in the grace of God bearing the fruits of righteousness.

Galatians 5:16 says *"This I say then, Walk in the Spirit, and ye shall not fulfil the lust of the flesh."* By this we understand that when we walk in the spirit of God we have power over our bodies and sin. The more we submit to the Holy Spirit and its leading the more we see the fruits of liberty in our lives.

It is a sad thing to see people embrace Jesus Christ and his Holy Spirit and turn away back into the world. Usually when people do this there are aspects of the flesh or their past life that they are not willing to give up and so when the Holy Spirit begins to challenge every part of their being and try to influence change, they block God out and hold onto things. Their inner desire is to have God according to their own lifestyles choices. We have to understand that there can be no combination of the old and the new. When the Holy Spirit comes into your life he desires that you be brand new. 2 Corinthians 5:17 says, *"Therefore if any man be in Christ, he is a new creature: old things are passed away; behold, all things are become new."*

Binding the Strongman

There are many people that truly want to be free from spiritual oppression. Some people that are desperate for healing and deliverance don't ever truly get free because they are not attempting to be delivered from the source of the oppression. Jesus said in Matthew 12:29, *"Or else how can one enter into a strong man's house, and spoil his goods, except he first bind the strong man? and then he will spoil his house. "* A strongman in the spirit is evil spirit that rules a person's life. This strong man spirit usually enters in because of some sin or offense that a person is not willing to let go of. This spirit will become the gate keeper to a person's life and invites other spirits to come and live with it inside a person.

When people wrestle with issues that they are having in their lives they usually look at the present issue that they are having. For instance a person that smokes cigarettes may be trying to quit. They pray to stop smoking and try many things to stop, but the issue keeps coming back. Their problem is that they are not dealing with the root cause of the smoking addiction. They may be nervous because they were in an accident or they had trouble in their marriage or any number of other issues. These situations may causes them to seek to relax by smoking. In these cases the strongman may be fear or anxiety, but if they only focus on the addiction, they may never get free from the thing that really plagues them.

True liberty comes through going after the source of a problem. When the strongman is removed from his position of ruling over your spiritual house, all the weaker inhabitants leave immediately. For this reason many times the strong man spirit will try to keep its presence hidden. It could have entered a person's life decades prior. It will try to get you to fight and fight to be free of the wrong thing until it wears you out. This draining of a person's determination to resist often times leads to an acceptance of the things they can't get free from. Once a person has embraced their problems as impossible to overcome, they have given this strongman full authority over their life.

When I minister to people about their situations, I often ask them about childhood and early adult experiences. Many times it is determined that there were things that were experienced that the individual had forgotten about. Many times the acknowledging of things hidden from the past opens the door to forgiveness and healing from past hurts. People have a natural way of building defense mechanisms against things that hurt them in life. These mechanisms are not always good, but to the hurt person it may seem reasonable to avoid more hurt. Individuals who want to be truly liberated in Jesus Christ, have let go of their own built up defenses and allow the spirit of God to bring defense. When God carries your burdens it will always bring peace and rest to your life.

FREE FROM CAPTIVITY

Chapter 5
The Abundant Life

John 10:10 *"The thief cometh not, but for to steal, and to kill, and to destroy: I am come that they might have life, and that they might have it more abundantly."*

Filling the Cup

God desires that we have an abundant life. This abundance comes through our relationship with Jesus Christ and the indwelling of his holy spirit. It is clear through this scripture that the devil wants to make your life miserable and spiritually unproductive and that God desires your life to be spiritually full of good things. The definition of abundant is "to have a plentiful supply or to have a lot. Life is a quality that distinguishes something from being a dead body, spiritually it can be said that it is an existence that is external. When Jesus said that he came that we may have an abundant life he was saying we could experience the fullness of relationship with him in this life and in the next. In the simple terms when we enter a relationship with Christ we are eternally blessed.

The abundant life in Jesus Christ gives us power over sin and the desires of our flesh. It opens the door for the purpose of God to be established in our life. Christ's abundance even brings peace and solitude in the middle of the most trying situations. Isaiah 26:3 says," *thou wilt keep him in perfect peace, whose mind is stayed on thee: because he trusted in thee"*.

Our abundance in Jesus Christ is an overflow of the Holy Spirit in our lives. Romans 8:9-10, *" But ye are not in the flesh, but in the Spirit, if so be that the Spirit of God dwell in you. Now if any man have not the Spirit of Christ, he is none of his. And if Christ be in you, the body is dead because of sin; but the Spirit is life because of righteousness."* To see the abundance of Jesus Christ's power in your life you must have the indwelling power of his spirit. Before Jesus went to the cross he told his disciples that they would do greater works because he was going to heaven to be with God. When he said this he was talking about the power of the Holy Spirit in him being distributed to his followers. With Jesus Christ's spirit being distributed across the world it magnifies his power. The bible says in the last days that God will pour out his spirit on all flesh. This distribution of Gods power leads to an abundance of his glory in this life.

Our relationship with Jesus, is powered by the Holy Spirit, and we cannot receive salvation without it. . In Romans 8:9 is says *"But ye are not in the flesh, but in the Spirit, if so be that the Spirit of God dwell in you. Now if any man have not the Spirit of Christ, he is none of his."* Our interaction with him at the point of salvation opens the door to overcome all things that are against us in this life. It is obvious through scripture that the filling of God's Holy Spirit is essential to live a life well pleasing to him. Once we receive salvation the Holy Spirit begins to develop us into a place of receiving the fullness of his spirit. The fullness of the Holy Spirit is a perfected and complete work within a person. It is a place of authority and power in the spirit.

<u>Putting On the Whole Armor of God</u>

I have met a lot of people that have been Christians for various amounts of time but still don't have a grasp of what it really means to put on the Armor of God. The confusion can open the door for doubt, frustration, and the creation of a false reality. When I got saved I thought that after I believed in Jesus and cut sin out of my life, everything would be perfect. I thought that everyone would respect my choice and kind of look up to me living for Jesus. I had no idea what I was in store for. I spent the first year of my Christian life crying and pleading to God for help and understanding. It got so bad I started to question why I chose to live for Jesus in the first place. The spirit of God had to reveal to me that I was a soldier for Jesus Christ and that God had called me to fight for his kingdom. The abundant life that Jesus promised me was a position of authority to overcome the works of evil and establish good in my life and the lives of others.

Ephesians 6:11-13 says, *"Put on the whole armour of God, that ye may be able to stand against the wiles of the devil. For we wrestle not against flesh and blood, but against principalities, against powers, against the rulers of the darkness of this world, against spiritual wickedness in high places. Wherefore take unto you the whole armour of God, that ye may be able to withstand in the evil day, and having done all, to stand."* It is obvious that if you don't have the revelation of the need to fight, then you won't be able to with stand the onslaught of the devil. Many times we look at our natural circumstances and don't see a need to fight. Our battle is not in the natural. It is spiritual. It says that we don't wrestle with flesh and blood meaning that men and mankind are not our ultimate enemies. Our true enemies reside in the realm of the spirit. It says we fight against principalities, powers, rulers of darkness, and spiritual wickedness in high places. These places are demonic hierarchies in the spirit realm. The influence and infestation of evil in this world comes from these places. When we are in a full relationship with Jesus Christ we have the ability to fight and win against any evil devices.

As any soldier there is an equipping that God gives us through his spirit. It says in Ephesians 6:14-17 *"Stand therefore, having your loins girt about with truth, and having on the breastplate of righteousness; And your feet shod with the preparation of the gospel of peace; Above all, taking the shield of faith, wherewith ye shall be able to quench all the fiery darts of the wicked. And take the helmet of salvation, and the sword of the Spirit, which is the word of God:"* There are 6 pieces of equipment we need to be effective as soldiers in the spirit. They are the belt of truth, the breastplate of righteousness, shoes of peace, the shield of faith, the helmet of salvation, and the sword of the spirit.

1. Helmet of Salvation

The Helmet of Salvation is a protector of the soul. Your soul is your eternal life force that resides in your body. Your soul is the part of you that will transition from this life to the next. It is where all the decisions are made. Your soul embodies the mind which is the control center of the body. Without it the body cannot function. It is no wonder that since this is the place that you choose to serve Jesus Christ that it needs to be guarded and protected. When the bible instructs us to put on the Helmet of Salvation it is saying that when we choose Christ we guard our mind/soul and secure it for eternity. The bible says that we are transformed by the renewing of our minds. This transformation gives us the mind of Christ. The mind of Christ is a renewed sense of reality and way of thinking powered by the Holy Spirit. It says in Romans 12:2 *"And be not conformed to this world: but be ye transformed by the renewing of your mind, that ye may prove what is that good,*

and acceptable, and perfect, will of God."
    We put on the helmet of Salvation by following Romans 10:9, *"That if thou shalt confess with thy mouth the Lord Jesus, and shalt believe in thine heart that God hath raised him from the dead, thou shalt be saved."*

2. Belt of truth

    If you don't wear a belt your pants will begin to sag and for some they may fall down. When your garment falls around your ankles it is very difficult to walk. Most would stumble and become completely inefficient with moving around. Our liberty is found in our ability to walk in the things of God. It is a freedom in the spirit. When we have the belt of truth we walk in a liberated place. In John 8:32 it says, *"And ye shall know the truth, and the truth shall make you free. "* If you live a lie, you will always be lead into destruction. A person's breakthrough could be tied to them walking through a particular door, but if they don't know the door exists or that breakthrough is on the other side, then how can they know to go through it.   Knowing that Jesus came to set the captives free puts the believer in a place of having absolute assurance of who they are in Jesus Christ and the promises that are afforded to them.

3. Breastplate of Righteousness

1 John 3:7 *"Little children, let no man deceive you: he that doeth righteousness is righteous, even as he is*

righteous."

Most of your vital organs are located in the chest area. It is no wonder that we are instructed to put on the breastplate of Righteousness. Without your vital organs, your body cannot function. Without living according to the will of God we are not justified before him and cannot live in the spirit. Righteousness is the state of being and doing holiness. Romans 10:10 says *"For with the heart man believeth unto righteousness;"* ...Meaning that if we love God then we will do his words. Jesus said if a man loves him he will keep his commands. We put on the breastplate by doing the will of God.

4. Shoes Of Gospel Of Peace

1 Jonn 1:7 *"But if we walk in the light, as he is in the light, we have fellowship one with another, and the blood of Jesus Christ his Son cleanseth us from all sin."*

Shoes are worn so you won't get hurt when you walk over tough and dangerous surfaces. Not having proper foot wear can cause pain and trouble in many parts of your body. When we put of the shoes of the Gospel of peace, we find rest and comfort while serving God. Our walk in life is guided by our labor in his word. Romans says 10:15 says *"How beautiful are the feet of them that preach the gospel of peace, and bring glad tidings of good things!"*.

5. Shield Of Faith

Ephesians 6:16 *"Above all, taking the shield of faith, wherewith ye shall be able to quench all the fiery darts of the wicked."*

Faith is what gives you the ability to resist all the doubts, bad experiences, and fears that cause you to run. Faith is as the bible says the substance of things hoped for, the evidence of things not seen. It is believing without seeing, knowing that what you can't see is real, because it's what you believe. Faith gives us supernatural access to the power of God. Without it we cannot fend off the pressures of Satan. It is given as a shield because it represents a resistance to every evil word spoken against God's will and direction in your life.

The bible says that without faith it impossible to please God. This means that we must live a lifestyle of believing God for everything. As a defense tool, faith keeps Satan and all his tactics away from you. If you don't have the shield of faith, your other pieces of armor won't last long. Your victory and reward in all battles comes from having faith.

Faith is not just a belief, it is an action. You cannot say you have faith in something if you don't act in a way that confirms what you say you believe. When young David in the bible saw the Giant Goliath waiting for someone to fight he was not afraid. He knew that God was more powerful than Goliath. As David looked at Goliath he wondered who this person was that would dare speak against God. As David approached Goliath the bible says that he was running

with full confidence that Goliath would be defeated.
Faith is a condition of being convinced. If you have to think about it, you are not in faith. We take up the shield of faith with full confidence that every attack of the devil will be stopped.

6. Sword Of The Spirit

Hebrews 4:12 *"For the word of God is quick, and powerful, and sharper than any twoedged sword, piercing even to the dividing asunder of soul and spirit, and of the joints and marrow, and is a discerner of the thoughts and intents of the heart."*

The sword of the spirit is our main weapon to fight the devil, without it we would be unable to wage a meaningful attack against evil spirits. We are equipped with this sword through the written word and the spoken word. We have the written word of God in our bibles. It tells us who God is, who we are, how we are to live, and how to overcome the enemy. Enclosed in the word of God are the promises of God and testimonies to strengthen our faith in the time of trouble. We also have the spoken word of God whether it is given by prophecy, revelation, or interpretation. These also are effective tools of Christians.
Jesus showed the power of the word of God when he first began his ministry. After he had been baptized the bible said he was led by the spirit of God into the wilderness. After he had fasted for forty days Satan tried to tempt him three times. It says in Matthew 4:2-4 *" And when he had fasted forty days*

and forty nights, he was afterward an hungred. And when the tempter came to him, he said, If thou be the Son of God, command that these stones be made bread. But he answered and said, It is written, Man shall not live by bread alone, but by every word that proceedeth out of the mouth of God. " Jesus effectively used the word of God to refute Satan's temptations. After he saw that Jesus was using the word, Satan refines his tactics, he comes to Jesus to tempt him through the word. It says in Matthew 4:5-7, *"Then the devil taketh him up into the holy city, and setteth him on a pinnacle of the temple, And saith unto him, If thou be the Son of God, cast thyself down: for it is written, He shall give his angels charge concerning thee: and in their hands they shall bear thee up, lest at any time thou dash thy foot against a stone. Jesus said unto him, It is written again, Thou shalt not tempt the Lord thy God."* Again Jesus fights him back with the word of God. If you are not efficient in the word of God, Satan will try to use it to trick you into sinning. The third time Satan approached Jesus he attacked him with same temptation that led to his own fall. It says in Matthew 4:8-10, *"Again, the devil taketh him up into an exceeding high mountain, and sheweth him all the kingdoms of the world, and the glory of them; And saith unto him, All these things will I give thee, if thou wilt fall down and worship me. Then saith Jesus unto him, Get thee hence, Satan: for it is written, Thou shalt worship the Lord thy God, and him only shalt thou serve."* Jesus fought off the temptation of the devil with the word of God. Satan tempted Jesus with pride and power. It is the temptation that enters and overtakes many people's hearts, but Jesus overcame it with the word of God.

If we keep the word of God in our hearts then everything that comes against us will have to submit to it. It is the final word in all situations. Through God's word the heavens and the earth were formed. If God said it, you can count on it. The bible says in Numbers 23:19, *"God is not a man, that he should lie; neither the son of man, that he should repent: hath he said, and shall he not do it? or hath he spoken, and shall he not make it good?"* The reason why Gods word is so powerful is that nothing can stop it. It's that sword that makes the impossible possible.

Prayer & Tongues

Everything that we have in this life that has eternal value is tied to our relationship with Jesus Christ. If we have a good relationship then we gain access to the blessings of the spirit. If we have a bad relationship then we will find ourselves cutoff from the spirit of God.

In order to have a good relationship with God, one of the key things is to have regular communication with him. Communication establishes relationships. This relationship comes through an active prayer life. When the bible instructs us to pray without ceasing it is saying that our praying should become a lifestyle. Prayer time is not negotiable when you want divine understanding and assistance in life. It is our prayers to God that make petitions for all our needs, it gives us the opportunity to commune with Jesus, and to establish ourselves in the body of Christ.

Prayer comes in two forms:
1. Prayer in our own language
2. Prayer in the spirit (unknown tongue)

There are many examples of prayer in the bible. You can read and pray these prayers when you are going through problems. You pray these prayers when you know what you are going through. Jesus prayed specifically about his having to go through the cross. He knew that he was going to have to die on the cross and so he prayed God's will in the matter. When you are aware of the present or future trials that you are facing, spending time with God in prayer can only help. If it is to get peace in the middle of your life's storm or just thanking God for who he is. Your prayers go a very long way.

In the bible story of Job, terrible things happened in his life. Bad things didn't happen because he was a bad man, but because Satan was trying to show God that when afflictions happen, people turn from God. Satan killed jobs servants, his cattle, and his children. As these disasters happened at the same time, Job, being a righteous man, didn't get angry with God. He shaved his head and gave God the glory. I always remind people of this story because sometimes we forget that we have an adversary and pray to God in anger or frustration for our situations. The bible says that Job did not blame

God foolishly but worshipped him.

Our prayers before God should always open with a heart of repentance and thanksgivings. The bible says we should enter his gates with thanksgiving. We should not pray to God with anger, offense, accusation, pride, covetousness, etc. We should pray to God in faith seeking his will in every situation. When you pray in this way you open the door for God to answer your prayers.

The power of our prayers is unlimited. James 5:16 states, *"The effectual fervent prayer of a righteous man availeth much"*. This is basically saying when we pray powerfully all the time to God, much happens. My grandfather used to pray for rain for his crops and it would rain. Earnest prayers of righteous men and women compels God to move in all situations. It says in James 5:17-18 *" Elias was a man subject to like passions as we are, and he prayed earnestly that it might not rain: and it rained not on the earth by the space of three years and six months. And he prayed again, and the heaven gave rain, and the earth brought forth her fruit."* Your prayers have the power to stop every bad situation according to the will of God.

Every major move I have made in ministry I prayed to God first about it. When I would act on his direction, amazing things would happen. David said, *"As for me, I will call upon God; and the LORD shall save me. Evening, and morning, and at noon, will I pray, and cry aloud: and he shall hear my voice."* (Psalms 55:16-17) Through sickness, trouble, misunderstandings, etc., prayer will always be an escape hatch. The bible says the prayer of faith will save the sick. When we pray to God we pray believing that he is hearing our prayers and moving on our behalf.

Praying in the Spirit (unknown tongue)

People like to know everything that they are going to have to deal with in life, unfortunately we will not be able to see every trial and tribulation that comes our way. Sometimes we just don't know we need prayer in certain areas. Our lack of knowledge on future things puts us in a position of having to rely on God. This is why we should seek to pray in the spirit. Praying in the spirit is a supernatural process of allowing the Holy Spirit to pray for you. Romans 8:26 says, *"Likewise the Spirit also helpeth our infirmities: for we know not what we should pray for as we ought: but the Spirit itself maketh intercession for us with groanings which cannot be uttered."* The spirit knows all things and when it prays it makes intercession for things we would never know about. 1 Corinthians 14:14 says, *"For if I pray in an unknown tongue, my spirit prayeth, but my understanding is unfruitful."*

It takes faith to pray in an unknown tongue. You have to believe that the spirit of God is praying through you. If you think that it is a waste of time or useless then you will not see the benefits of having a supernatural intercessor.

Many years ago I was taking a plane trip for business. As most large airports are busy, there was a delay between me getting on the plane and the plane getting into the air. I was in the plane sitting on the runway behind ten other planes, when the spirit of God told me to start to pray in the spirit. I had no idea what was going on but I did as the spirit of God instructed. I thought that maybe God was trying to calm my nerves by having me to pray in tongues while we waited on runway. I probably was sitting there in the plane praying for about an hour when our turn came to take off. The spirit of God was insistent that I continue praying. As the plane accelerated down the runway we approached take off speed. All of a sudden the pilot slammed on the brakes of the plane and we turned off the runway. He came over the speaker and said that the airplanes engine had failed and if we had taken off then we would have crashed. I will always have that testimony of how the spirit of God saved me that day through the power of the spiritual tongue.

Power of Love

There is no greater power than the power of love. It is the foundation for everything we do for God. It says in Ephesians 3:19 *"And to know the love of Christ, which passeth knowledge, that ye might be filled with all the fulness of God."* It was the power of love that had Jesus die on the cross for our sins. Love breaks barriers. It has people go where they said they would never go. It will cause grown men to trade in everything for it. The bible says that without it we are nothing. Nothing else matters to God unless we have love in our hearts.

Our first commandment is to love God and our

second is to love our neighbors as ourselves. These two requirements are not negotiable. It is the fertile ground from which everything else flows. The bible says that God searches the hearts of men. He is looking at the intents of the heart. If your intents are in love then God will bless it.

We are instructed by God to love everyone. It can be easy to love on friends or close family members but many times people have a hard time loving on people that they don't know or are enemies. It doesn't matter who someone is or how they have treated you. Our love as Christians goes higher than a condition because it is unconditional. When our love is unconditional it overcomes any evil that comes our way. Jesus overcame death and the cross with love. Even at the point of death, Jesus spoke forgiveness over the ones who had put him on the cross.

When we live to love on our fellow man, we live in God's abundance. There is a supernatural peace that flows in a heart filled with love. The bible says that while all other things may cease, love will never fail.

FREE FROM CAPTIVITY

Keys to a Greater Love Walk:

1. Know that God loved us before we were even born (1 John 4:19)

2. Help others achieve things that you don't have (John 15:13)

3. Pray for your enemies   (Matthew 5:44)

4. Help your enemies (Matthew 5:40)

5. Tell people about Jesus Christ (James 5:20)

6. Follow Gods direction for our life (John 14:23)

7. Love others as much as yourself (Romans 13:9)

FREE FROM CAPTIVITY

Chapter 6
Purposed to Pour into Others

Rom 8:28 "And we know that all things work together for good to them that love God, to them who are the called according to his purpose."

Life can be so uncertain and difficult that many times people find themselves constantly trying to work things out. They work hard trying to make sure that they are going to be ok. It can be easy to fall into a mindset of just worrying about yourself. One of the quickest things I've learned in ministry is that it is not just about you. Your growth and liberty in Christ is directly tied to how you bless others with what God has given you. Sometimes even the breakthrough people are looking for is hinged upon them helping someone else. Every person filled with God's Holy Spirit becomes a light in a spiritually dark world. This light is meant to shine that others may find the light of Christ.

When we become children of God, we become disciples of Jesus Christ. A disciple is a student and follower of Jesus Christ. Being a follower of Jesus Christ we look to him for direction and guidance on his will for our lives.

One of the commands Jesus gave to his original disciples was, *"Go therefore and make disciples of all the nations, baptizing them in the name of the Father and of the Son and of the Holy Spirit,"* Matthew 28:19. This call to disciple the nations is a generational direction from Jesus Christ. He knew that his initial twelve would not be able to take his message everywhere and that they would not be able to disciple everyone. He wanted them to find some people to disciple and build up and be strong enough to go out and disciple others themselves. This recreation of yourself in others extends your reach and allows you to impact many more than you could on your own. That's what Jesus did. He raised and trained his twelve disciples and sent them out to expand the work. From teaching the disciples, his message and teachings have reached around the world. Jesus was not assigned to travel around the world and teach and plant churches. It was the assignment for those that came after him. Jesus knew that the new work he was starting in his disciples would be generational. The bible calls him the first born of many brethren. He blessed us with his life and death to continue to carry on his work.

When God called me to start a church I was confused. There seemed like there was a church on every corner. I felt like there were many places for people to go and grow in Jesus Christ. I asked him why we needed another church, he said "because my people are suffering". I understand now why he told me to start a work. There are so many souls that are wondering around not having any spiritual direction about them. They are spiritual nomads, some having tried to attend church before, others just never giving a commitment to God a serious thought.

The bible says that the harvest is plenteous but the laborers are few. This means that there are many people that need direction on how to follow after Jesus, but not many that are willing to lead them into that place. If you are a Christian then you are called to be a disciple of Jesus Christ. Being a disciple you should strive to disciple of others.

To be a disciple to others doesn't mean you have to be a pastor in your church. It doesn't even mean you have to be on the leadership team at your church. It just means you are strong enough in your own walk with Christ to be able to stop focusing so much on yourself and help others to become stronger in the things of God. The same way a big brother or sister helps their little brother or sister. The disciple of Christ looks after those that are weaker in faith.

Scripture says that God is looking for you to be faithful in what he has given. This faithfulness translates into using the gifts that God has given you to bless others. Jesus is our example for how we are to disciple others. He said in John 15:13, *"Greater love hath no man than this, that a man lay down his life for his friends."* Jesus called them friends, taught them, then he went to the cross to die for them. We should follow his example of fellowship, teaching, and sacrificing ourselves so that others may grow. A true disciple wants nothing more than the ones that he is leading to excel.

    It shouldn't matter if you have one person to disciple or 10,000. You should put as much effort in as possible. Some people only put an effort in when they think they can have a large impact. Its not about the quantity to God, it's about being faithful in what he has given.

    One teaching that Jesus spoke on in relation to faithfulness was the parable of the talents. In this story it says that the Lord had given out talents to his servants. One received five talents, one received two talents, and the other received one talent. The servant that received the five talents worked hard and earned five more talents. The servant that had received two talents worked hard and earned two more talents. The servant that had received one went and buried the talent that he had. When the lord returned to see how his servants had done, he was happy with those who had gotten a large return but disappointed with the one that had buried their talent. God does not want us take what he has given us and bury it. He wants us to take what he has given us and use it to bless his people.

    Every one of us that truly lives for Jesus Christ has a calling to disciple others. You can find a friend at work and help them, you can start a small bible study, you can join a group at church, you can be that voice of inspiration to your personal friends and family. Jesus only had twelve and he was faithful in what God had given him.

      Sometimes Christians can become disheartened because they don't feel like they have any impact on people or the people that they were ministering to fell off. Jesus encountered the same trouble and resistance in his ministry. One day Jesus was ministering to some people. He had gathered a large following because of the mighty works that he had done. When Jesus began to teach them about his holy communion, the crowds of people became offended with Jesus and left him alone with his original disciples. It was such a dramatic departure that Jesus even asked his disciples if they were going to leave also.

      As followers of Christ we cannot allow what we see or experience with people affect us. We must continue to follow the will of God. Everyone might not follow or go in the direction that you are going, but as long as you are doing the will of God, your work is blessed.

FREE FROM CAPTIVITY

Chapter 7
Dead Weight

Galatians 5:1 "Stand fast therefore in the liberty wherewith Christ hath made us free, and be not entangled again with the yoke of bondage."

    We have many times heard the terminology dead weight and even the term emotional baggage. These are words that describe someone or something that we carry with us that is hurtful or hindering to progress that we may be able to make with some situation. We have all had dead weight in our lives or know someone who has carried a weight around with them. These weights can manifest themselves in many ways. They can come from emotions, people, desires, debt, etc. Spiritually these weights can choke out any growth or liberty we can find in Jesus Christ.
    One of the hardest parts of living a liberated life in Christ is staying liberated. Even though our

relationship with Christ sets us free, devils and our flesh often times will temp us to go back to a place of bondage and despair. After a person goes backward they often times find themselves in a worse place than when they started. Jesus said it best when he said in Luke 11:24-26, *"When the unclean spirit is gone out of a man, he walketh through dry places, seeking rest; and finding none, he saith, I will return unto my house whence I came out. And when he cometh, he findeth it swept and garnished. Then goeth he, and taketh to him seven other spirits more wicked than himself; and they enter in, and dwell there: and the last state of that man is worse than the first."* When you hold on to things or go back to things that cannot benefit you in your spiritual walk with Christ, there is only one result and that's finding yourself back in captivity. One of the most obvious dead weights is the continuance of sin once you have chosen to live for Jesus Christ. To be in sin is to be dead in the spirit and to be in the spirit is to be dead to sin. So it is reasonable to say that sin is a dead weight to living for Jesus Christ.

      In most Christian teachings the issue of sin is well taught and people often times work hard to navigate living righteously and holy before God. God showed me that there was a need to also teach on some dead weights that are less obvious but plague the body of Christ. The weights that are very damaging spiritually but not spoke of as much are people, positions, and prophecies.

<u>People</u>
      When I first ventured out into living for Jesus

Christ. I was excited about telling people about my salvation and what God had done for me. I quickly realized that a lot of people needed encouragement and spiritual direction. Many people inside and outside of churches are to some extent searching and trying to understand their journey with God. I was so excited to encourage them and give them my testimony and the things that I learned. As I went along my journey telling people about living for Christ I started to see a trend....many people would selectively listen to what I told them according to what they were trying to hear. I would tell them about how God blessed me and they would embrace that. When I talked about leaving sin the conversation would go the other route. Many people were segmenting God according to what they felt needed to be fixed and leaving the other in place. Even the people I would meet in church. I would see people sitting on the front row of church and jumping up excited for God, then disperse pornography among friends the next day. I met a woman who was going to a church I attended at the time. She was extremely active in the church, but would sleep with different men in church and would talk about them if they were trying to live righteously.

  These hypocritical situations I kept running into made me a lot more cautious about who I spent a lot of time with ministering to. Many times when a person tries to help people grow in God, Satan will send individuals who will never change, never grow, and never get to a place of liberty. Loving God and loving his people, many will wear themselves out trying to convince someone of something that they don't want. I know stories of people running out to save someone in dire situations and once they get free they turn around and put themselves in the same situations the next week over. After a while a cycle gets started….They continue in evil, they fall into a snare, someone saves them, then they fall into the same snare, that someone saves them again. This cycle can snare the believer that wants to help and cause them to go into captivity themselves or to stop trying to minister and save people.

<u>Purpose</u>

The issue of spiritual dead weights can even go into finding purpose. Many times we want our friends, family, associates to come with us when we take journeys, but many times we find that people close to us don't have the same energy and desire that we have for the journey. When God gives a person purpose in life, he assigns it to them as an individual. All Christians are a part of the body of Christ, but have different functions. It says in 1 Corinthians 12:14-18 *"For the body is not one member, but many. If the foot shall say, Because I am not the hand, I am not of the body; is it therefore not of the body? And if the ear shall say, Because I am not the eye, I am not of the body; is it therefore not of the body? If the whole body were an eye, where were the hearing? If the whole were hearing, where were the smelling? But now hath God set the members every one of them in the body, as it hath pleased him."* Our purpose is what makes us unique in the body of Christ. For instance the foot has one function in the body and the eye has another function. Both work together but the eye can't do what the foot does and the foot can't do what the eye does. When you have purpose every one can't roll with your assignment. They don't have the revelation for it and they are not equipped for it. To carry them on your purpose would be the same as taking pillow to a sword fight. When you carry people on your purpose who God has not designated, it can lead you into captivity. Your your energy will end of being spent trying to convince and motivate someone who does not have the grace for your task. Their lack of strength and enthusiasm may even convince you that you have taken on the wrong purpose.

<u>Positions</u>

It is a great thing to know that God has a plan and purpose for us. Many times people know there is a purpose but they don't know what that purpose is. When I first started to try and understand what God wanted me to do as a minister, I read a book on the fivefold ministry. I found myself critiquing the different positions trying to figure out which one I wanted to do. I felt at the time that the office of a teacher was the leadership vocation I was called into and I made up in my mind that I was going to teach. Shortly after that the spirit of God, told me to find a warehouse. I wasn't sure about the details but was excited because the lord was starting a work in me! I went out daily and searched for a space and finally found where God had ordained me to start my work. I opened the doors of the church soon after expecting a surge of people and mighty work to unfold. I said to myself that I must be a pastor also because I have a church and I am going to be sheparding people. I thought to myself that I was a pastor/teacher. As I started having services, people would visit but no one would join. Some would come with dire financial needs and we would help them and they would move on. After a year of preaching and teaching we still didn't have any committed members and I started to question whether or not God had called me into ministry. As the time went on I started sitting in my office looking out the window on Sunday morning to see if anyone was going to show up. I would become frustrated when no one would show up and It began to drag me emotionally down. When the finances started getting low and the attendance had not changed over that time, I began to think to myself that there was something missing. I couldn't quite put my finger on it, but I knew that something had to change. After I had talked to a pastor friend of mine about my churches financial issues and low attendance, he extended me the opportunity to come and use his church at no charge. I jumped on the opportunity. I closed my church location down and moved to the new location. When I got there I thought to myself that things were going to be different. Unfortunately we continued to have small services with very low attendance. One day after church an Apostle friend said to me, "you know you are not a pastor, right". I looked at him and he just looked at me. Something about those words resonated with me. Maybe I wasn't a pastor, but why did God have me start this work. I started studying about the office of the Apostle and realized that God used them to start works and establish churches. Previously when I had studied that office, it wasn't something that seemed interesting to me. My Apostle friend started talking to me about the signs of an Apostle. I could see all of them in my life. As I prayed deeply about it, God confirmed it in my life.

Once I had embraced being an Apostle, God began to change the dynamics of the church. He told me to start having Thursday night services and Sunday bible study. After the services started, we began to see a great move of God. People started to come and join the church and most of them were built to work in Apostolic ministry.

I told you this story for you to understand that being out of position can be a detriment to the purpose that God has for your life. When God calls you for a purpose he equips you for that purpose. If you do something outside of Gods plan you usually will find yourself unprepared for the task. Many people have taken on positions in the church that God has not called them to take on. They take them on not understanding who they are and by doing so put themselves into bondage. There is a grace that goes with being aligned with God. Weights and burdens are different when they are yours to bear. When they are not yours to bear it will drag you into a hole.

Prophecies

Every loves to get an accurate word from the lord. Life is so difficult and our search for understanding can be eased by a word directly from the Lord. What's going to happen next? When am I going to get married? What business move should I make? Will I ever get out of debt?....These are some of the questions people have for prophets and they are more than over joyed to run with the prophetic words that are given to them. People will hinge their whole life on a word given to them, not really being able to discern if it is from God or from something else. The bible says that prophecy is for edification, exhortation, and comfort. True prophecies from God can lead to peace and liberty. False prophecies can lead to a life in spiritual captivity. When the Apostle Paul was out preaching a woman with a spirit of divination approached him. She began to say good things about his ministry and tell the people that they needed to follow him. Paul was irritated by her and casted the devil out of her. If Paul had not been discerning he would have embraced her because she had good things to say about his ministry. If he had allowed her to be apart of his work, she certainly would have ruined his ministry. Her prophecies would have been straight from hell.

    Most of the time when a prophecy goes out it is continually confirmed out of multiple prophets and within the persons own spirit. Random prophecies with no other confirmation should be seriously prayed about.

    Many years ago I was at a prophecy conference and the host prophet for the conference brought all the leaders up to the front of the room. He said that he didn't have time to prophecy to all of the leaders but he had one that God had given a word for. He was talking to me. He said that the spirit of God had showed him that one of the families in my church was a cancer to the church and if I wanted to see growth in the church I needed to get rid of this family and then I would see growth in my church. The whole prophecy was foolishness because at the time I didn't have any members at my church. This guy was a false prophet. The scary part is that I think about if I had had some members at that time I may have been looking for that cancer in the church. These types of false words can lead to long term frustration and confusion. When a false word is given, the more they hold on to the prophecy the worse things get.

    False words get trapped in the soul of a person and can literally paralyze their growth in Christ. These false words are designed to keep men and women of God in a state of confusion and lack of fulfillment. Jezebel spirits masquerade as prophets of the lord, but when they actuality speak only words of divination come out. Jezebel is a master of binding the spiritual growth and authority of a believer.

    Every time I read the story of Elijah and the woman Jezebel it amazes me how one word from her caused Elijah to run away hoping to die. Elijah was a mighty prophet for God, who was destroying all the Enuchs of Jezebel. When she found out what he was doing, she sent him a message prophesying that he would be dead by the next day. Elijah being fearful ran into the wilderness and asked God if he could die. Many false prophets will speak a word from Jezebel and strike fear in the hearts of men and women of God. Beware of false prophets that speak lies over your life.

FREE FROM CAPTIVITY

Chapter 8
Fruits Of Liberty

John 15:8 "Herein is my Father glorified, that ye bear much fruit; so shall ye be my disciples."

Being Children of God and heirs to an eternal kingdom, we can be certain that liberty in the spirit is guaranteed and absolute. Jesus didn't come that we may be halfway free or partially victorious over sin. He came that we may have complete power over sin and live victoriously in this life.
    This newly found liberated life brings you into a place of peace and rest in his spirit. A place were all the troubles in the world don't matter because Jesus is carrying all your burdens. With this new found freedom you see into the spirit better and even assist

others that need assisting. It becomes obvious that your liberty in the things of God wasn't as much about you as it was you helping others. The blindness that you once had becomes clear vision and the path you walk serves as a light for others to follow. As you see clearer you are able to operate in the spirit and produce the fruits of God in your life and the lives of others.

When Jesus was talking about knowing who the people of God were, he said that there was a key to recognizing them. He said in Matthew 7:17-20, "*Even so every good tree bringeth forth good fruit; but a corrupt tree bringeth forth evil fruit. A good tree cannot bring forth evil fruit, neither can a corrupt tree bring forth good fruit. Every tree that bringeth not forth good fruit is hewn down, and cast into the fire. Wherefore by their fruits ye shall know them.*" When it says fruit it is referring to the impact, effect, or influence that someone has on things. This good fruit produced is a result of someone being in a healthy state spiritually. When you are free in the spirit, fruits become abundant in your life. The bible tells us what these fruits should be. The fruits of the spirit are listed in Ephesians 5:9 & Galatians 5:22. The fruits of the spirit are righteousness, truth, love, joy, peace, longsuffering, gentleness, goodness, faith, Meekness, temperance.

God brought us into our liberty to be fruit bearers in his kingdom. You cannot bear fruit if you are in bondage. When you are free, fruit will abound in your life. God is even glorified in the fruit that you bring. It says in John 15:8, "*Herein is my Father glorified, that ye bear much fruit; so shall ye be my disciples."*

I have talked to many people that were experiencing confusion in their personal lives and ministerial lives and the one thing that I would always ask them is *"where's the fruit?"* The fruit is the signification that God is in it. Where there is no good fruit, there is no spirit of God. At the point of the Holy Spirit entering your life, fruit starts to be produced. When God is working in a situation the end result is always the fruit of God's spirit. Even in times of trouble his deliverance works patience and faith into your life. The bible says that the trying of your faith worketh (creates) patience. Every trial, tribulation, frustration allowed by God for his people creates a better, more perfected person who is even more liberated then they were before the struggle.

Jesus said in John 10:9, *"I am the door: by me if any man enter in, he shall be saved, and shall go in and out, and find pasture."* This pasture is a place of rest even in the middle of our storms. One of the scriptures that assures us of our rest in God is Psalms 23:1-6, *"The LORD is my shepherd; I shall not want. He maketh me to lie down in green pastures: he leadeth me beside the still waters. He restoreth my soul: he leadeth me in the paths of righteousness for his name's sake. Yea, though I walk through the valley of the shadow of death, I will fear no evil: for thou art with me; thy rod and thy staff they comfort me. Thou preparest a table before me in the presence of mine enemies: thou anointest my head with oil; my cup runneth over. Surely goodness and mercy shall follow me all the days of my life: and I will dwell in the house of the LORD forever."* We have to understand that even in our place of deepest trouble, God is still able to give us rest. There is no trouble too difficult and no situation too dire. Men will help you to avoid disaster, but not many will jump into the disaster with you.

A good example of God's ability to bring peace and comfort in the middle of tough times is the story of Shadrach, Meshach, and Abednego. These men were sentenced to death in a fiery furnace even though they were good and righteous men in God's eyes. They had refused to bow down to the false Gods of the king. The king was so angry that these men refused to worship his Gods that he turned the fire as hot as possible. When Shadrach. Meshach, and Abednego were thrown into the fire, the king was sure that they were killed. As he looked into the fire, he was shocked to find them walking around inside the fire. It shocked him even more that he saw a fourth man in the fire that looked like the son of God. When Shadrach, Meshach, and Abednego came out of the fire there wasn't a burn on them or their clothes.

Jesus has the power to give you rest in your darkest hour and deliver you out of that situation without a scratch. When the son of God sets you free, it's not halfway but a complete and final place.

FREE FROM CAPTIVITY

FREE FROM CAPTIVITY

Other books
by
James Alford

To order goto www.kingdomauthority.org

www.ingramcontent.com/pod-product-compliance
Lightning Source LLC
Chambersburg PA
CBHW060203050426
42446CB00013B/2978